a book of poetry

My Lovely, Lonely Mirror

LEILA & JULIA ESHAGHPOUR

eshtwinspoetry@gmail.com

ISBN: 978-1-09836-276-8 Print
ISBN: 978-1-09836-277-5 eBook

CONTENTS

In loving memory of our dear friend,
Nikan Baratian.
This poetry book is dedicated to the unbreakable bond
between his beautiful soul and his incredible twin sister,
Niki Baratian.

The world was made for two.

A Cautionary Prelude

Do not ask us if these poems are about you or him or her or
them. Poetry is about perspective; give it the light you desire.
Do not ask us for an explanation. Find the comfort to live
through these words yourself — the same words that have been
strung together by love and fear and lust and hate.
It is your story as much as it is ours.

• • •

We have decided to co-write this book for various reasons.
First, as a pair of identical twins, we felt that our words, pieced
together, would make for a more unique poetic experience.
Combining our thoughts into one work has allowed us to write
more authentically and in a manner that truly represents who
we are as a pair of poets. The goal of this work is to provide
our readers with a sense of comfort when life seems to become
too bleak. The poems — some written by both of us and some
written by just one of us — are an attempt to deeply explore
and question the darkness that can arise in our thoughts.
We hope it offers you some light on days that
may be too Black or Blue.

1

My Mirror

We observe our lives
In opposing mirrors
One black
One white

Which is real?
Which is right?
This is tough — we are in the gray
And the in-between dilutes our psyches

Sometimes they change colors
One day mine turned green
It was grotesque
The way my hair turned into slithering snakes

Another day yours turned yellow
This surprised me
I had never known you could see the light
And suddenly your eyes sparked with a new fire

There was one time I could recall
Where my mirror turned brown
It seeped into my blood
Slowed me down, and I craved a more delicate antidote

It was nice to have another mirror
To always complement my own
Considering we were made together
I had never questioned the parallels, never once thought to diverge
from the path we were always led on

But then came the day when my mirror shattered
Yours was left untouched, untarnished

And it was the same day I realized
I made the wrong turn

Or maybe the right one
But no matter
I was left in the snow on my own, you were left in the glistening
palm trees
In the blink of an eye, one split into two

Erratic

Keep coming back
Calmness is a foreigner

Perhaps this is how it should be
Ignorance coats the sad man

Narcissism stings
I laugh — It's wicked

A butterfly dies in my presence
The lukewarm water freezes

I bathe in my tears
Baptize my toes in coal

Lose myself in your erratic nothingness
Say goodbye to all sanity

It was a good run, my friend

The Idea of You

There is something quite
Empowering
About holding onto the pure possibility
Of someone

At the very least
It shows how hard it is to murder Hope

flesh and bones and irrevocable thoughts

we are born adorned with flesh and bones and irrevocable thoughts
they contort us in every which way they please
haunting us with beauty, consuming us with pain

your flesh and bones and lethal thoughts
they rot you from the inside out
distorting the image into one you could never stand

her flesh and bones and detestable thoughts
they infect the cells she once relied on
metamorphosing her brain into a personalized villain

his flesh and bones and perplexing thoughts
they hover over him as he stands on the edge of
each and every day
tantalizing the feeling of jumping off

but it's his flesh and bones and feasible thoughts
that help him take a step back from the ledge
granting him a chance to live the life he chooses to lead

it's her flesh and bones and invigorating thoughts
that guide her cells back to homeostasis
allowing the faintest outline of a smile to reappear on her lips

it's your flesh and bones and fantastical thoughts
that let you know that it is something of a privilege to dream
gifting you the power to move beyond the cracks of the mirror

what was once irrevocable becomes incomprehensible
flesh and bones amount to our final unceasing truths
we may only bear witness to our thoughts as they mutate
into the unforeseen light

Man-Made Destruction I

His glare pierced straight into your
Glimmering, golden eyes
With an empty hunger

There was something refreshing
About the truth his eyes told.
They screamed to your soul
"I need you"

You poor, naïve girl
He fed you words
Little by little
Building a time bomb of
The lovely life
That would soon follow

"Just wait for me beautiful,
Just wait"

You told him you would
He was what you needed:
A charismatic lover who would
Never fail to give you what you deserve

See, the problem with saying *yes,* my dear,
Is that you never realized
Being a mistress
Destroys a part of your soul

Yes is a loss of power
Yes means he has all the control

You cried the first time you said *yes*

You still waited, my dear
There is something nauseating
Or perhaps incredible
About blindly holding onto Hope

It was too late when you realized
The only reason he would never fail
To give you what you deserve
Is that he thought you deserved
Absolutely Nothing
His exquisitely crafted bomb
Detonated.
Debris scarred your pretty, little face

It took weeks for you to fathom the destruction
It took months for you to dissect

You discover that
His consuming stare
Had never been a tender expression of care;
It had simply meant
"I cannot wait to destroy you, my dear"

Fries & Burgers & Ice Cream

The words slid from her
Half-opened mouth
A snake crawled up my body
Every fiber of my being
Collapsed
Every thought in my frantic head
Convoluted
Overpowered
She
Said
It

It was the saddest news I had ever heard

It is unthinkable to fully swallow
But I've got to.
This is reality
This is the real world
This is not my dreams

But I am sorry
So very sorry, my love.
You are too delicate
An ivory rose
I am afraid
You'll
Crumble

Let us just eat the ice cream in peace
It is your birthday, after all

Cotton Candy

My eyes sting at the sight of the violently green golf course
We've arrived: the corporate giant and me,
his picture-perfect wife
It almost makes me miss the little boxes that we used to call home
This is a new America: one we've constructed, marketed,
and sold all by ourselves

I scour for an escape and force myself to look up
The off-white clouds intrigue me
I am seduced by their comfort
They make it seem as though a beautiful life is attainable
if I just …

Forced and trite small talk overtakes my fantasy
The rest of the flawless wives have entered the scene
I suppose that means that none of us must endure
this next escapade
All by ourselves

The men shed their covers: there is no longer a cotton
candy landscape
It is our cue to leave if we'd like to avoid the storm ahead
They revel in their testosterone
It is a concoction of bourbon, tobacco, and the grandiose ego
of a sick man

I am now forced to put the children to bed alone
Goodnight, my sweetheart
But mommy, can you tell me where daddy is?
Where does daddy always go so late?

I can only offer my silence in return
The raining stops

Here I am, cast under the spell of my own nightmares
In an attempt to evade my harsh realities with no luck

Sensory Intrusion, A Lovely Day Trip

The green speaks to me
It is the color I've been searching for my whole life
Every time I find it
I die a quick, painless death
Then am resurrected back to life

My body cannot bear the sight
An explosion in my chest overpowers me
Each time the sunlight illuminates the green
It is
So
Beautiful

Beauty violently erupts me
I can't take it anymore
Nothing matters and it's gorgeous
I embrace this
I free myself with this fresh breath of knowledge
And I love myself in a way formerly unknown to me

A sensory intrusion:
The sunlit green has invaded even the darkest of my thoughts
Oh, I think to myself
What a lovely day

Tree

I planted my roots inside of you
I grew with your every smile
You gifted me life in every moment

I never asked if you were okay with this
I never thought to
I have always considered you to be an implicit truth

Perhaps that is why my whole body aches
I was stabilized by the Idea of You
My roots were incredibly secured within your soul

Then, almost suddenly, they were not
They became excruciatingly afraid of the place they once called home
I became excruciatingly afraid

My roots were torn from their foundation
My life was mutilated by your ignorance
My limbs have gone limp

Desperation chokes me
Where is the person I once knew?
I hope this vacation is a short one

Endless Highways

We drive along the I-95 for hours
Silence engulfs me; it swallows me whole
I turn on the radio
A song I hate plays

If you'd ask me
I would say daydreaming is my favorite pastime
It is being awake
While not being awake at all

I imagine myself in a new life
Where I am named the powerful princess
I no longer wait for my prince
Because he is already there; he is always there

I replay my favorite scenario once again:
I am swaying with the dashing prince
We are intertwined; impossible to push apart
He gifts me a kiss so tender, yet so rough

I listen to the declaration
Of his endless love
To the most glorious woman
In all of the kingdoms near and far

Then I am jerked forward
I turn my head
And I am forced to unnaturally replace the perfect prince
With the man I am supposed to love

The pages have been brutally torn
The fairytale is skewed
The story is now a mere compilation of
The fluff between the scenes we never liked to read

the itsy, bitsy spider

i desire the warmth
that follows your touch
or is it the warmth that is supposed to follow?

i am caught up
in a very scary place

i do not like being tangled up
in your cryptic, convoluted web

it is blinding the itsy, bitsy spider
who tries to tiptoe her way
through this Great Awful World

Catching Happiness

There have been times
I've felt so
Empty
I forgot why I ever laughed
I forgot how smiling warms
The soul
I forgot what the Good
And I mean the *Really Good*
Feels likes
I forgot
How it feels to the touch
How its melody swoons me
How its aroma entrances me
There are times it all evades me
As I remind myself
To welcome the numbness with open arms

So, I sit and I wonder
Why am I drained of life?
Why am I so young yet so worn out?
Why am I beyond the reach of Happiness?
I try my best to understand

Happiness is simply what you construct:
It's the tiny compliment that makes your lips curl
It's the pretty flower you gaze at on the way to class
It's the new sliver of knowledge you've come across
That makes you wonder
How you ever possibly lived prior to this moment
Devoid of the beautiful information you have just learned

Happiness is what you feel
When your eyes

Pierce
Into the eyes of a person you care for
It is an all-consuming feeling
That leaves you no damn choice
But to smile
The most genuine smile you have ever known

Maybe you don't love them
But you feel something
You feel
Good

And again, I remember why I laughed

Condolences

There is no such thing
As finding solace
In another human being

It has been winter for a while now

Sadderdays

I could try to explain it to you
I think you could never understand
Not because I question your intelligence
Or your character
But because I am afraid you will begin
The period of resentment
That will inevitably follow

Your fuse tracks along for miles
Mine for inches
My mind exercises its strength
To retard the spark

I tell myself I have laser focus
To prevent the explosion
Or to at least slow it down

I know I do not

I think it is telling
How I am the monster on the stage
But you are the puppet master behind the velvet
Controlling my every move, my every thought

Over and over
They laugh
They sigh
They tell me to smile, you're so much prettier when you smile

I suppose they are blind
For it is obvious
I am granted no access
To the control-center of my mind

Permanent Disappearance

What are you
To do
When you hear
The most frightening
Paralyzing
Five words:
I want to kill myself

Do you give him a hug?
A kiss?
Do you tell him how much he means
To you?
To the world?
To you?

To his mother? To his father?
His sister? His brother?

I try to speak
But I am mute
I open my mouth
But there are no words I can allow right now

Only a hollow ghost exits through my weighted breaths
I can do nothing but
Stare

I am scared
I do not want to lose you
But I do not know how to save
A person
Who refuses to save
Himself

Sometimes you cannot
Cure someone
Who is sick

Like a man stranded at sea
The brain is convinced it must fight off the waves
All on its own

Sing Me to Sleep

We are zombies
There is a layer of smog
Veiling my thoughts
My vision is blurred

I consciously choose for this to deceive me

I am tired
In practically every sense

Tired of dreams
Tired of nightmares
Tired of the chalk
That clouds my judgement

I should sleep

You should sleep, they tell me
There is something distasteful
When they tell me: they know of the chaos ensuing in my head

Pinch me
I am awake

I am walking
I am running

Running from the jungle
The animals attacking
Get them out! Leave me be!

I am running I am running
I am swimming?

I suppose just wake me up when the snow has passed
And the mountains no longer glisten with the overwhelming
Layer of White

There's No Place Like Home

Uncertainty is the tornado
That has swooped up
And knocked little Dorothy
Out of her sparkling, ruby slippers

Something has rooted itself
Within my stomach
Something treacherous
Something unholy

I am convulsing
The foam flows
From my stained lips
I cannot think

I am unsure of this wave
Who leads it is beyond me
What it stands for I could almost tell you
But I cannot say Almost will ever help

The ivies trap me
Against the most picturesque landscape
There are so many doves
Too many doves

I wonder where I am
I do not know how my mind tricks me
But it always does
Always matters much more than Almost

I wait for the gatekeeper
I wonder where He'll let me in
I promise you
I try to be a Good Girl

I promise you
The fishnets do not mean much
But you can never keep your filthy hands
To your goddamn self

A flower blooms on my chest
I am no Eve
I am simply
The snake

Trying to click my heels together
I realize that, in the end
I'd just like to find my way home
Again

Like the Song

I write for myself to feel at ease
But I write for you to gain a glimpse
Of what I am capable of
I watch the leaves and hear their rustle
My head shifts up and I glance at your smile
I am at ease

But still, I only say I love you in my head
Over and over
Like the song
My little secret
Tucked deep inside my back pocket

I am at ease
But I am scared
Scared that you might think it too
Or scared that you might not
I do not know which would trouble me more

So, I keep it
In its safe spot
In my manic, rundown head
My favorite song
Stuck on repeat

I have to remember that this is all it is
I don't quite know if it's my own mind
Blocking a love from flourishing
Or my inherent instincts
That must know better
Than a fragile, little girl

Secondhand Smoke

It took six weeks
For my sheets to be
Baptized and cleansed
From your barbaric antics

It took nine weeks
For me to cultivate
A strong aversion
To the cigarette remnants lying on the street

It took twelve weeks
For me to start my longing period
I started to pray
I needed the cancerous smell

It took a year
For me to blossom
An aggressive hatred
Into a blood orange rose in my hair

Through it all, I suppose you can say
I learned about you and myself and the nature of emotions
But to what degree is this knowledge worth
The dark creatures gnawing my soul?

It is today I realize
No shred of knowledge
Can replace the way my heart
Melted into an ocean, only for you

An Adolescent Love Story

Maybe I never loved you
Maybe in the moment the words rolled off my tongue
All I wanted was reassurance
Happy security
A warm blanket embracing my numbness

My dear, if it is you
Who reads my uncompromising words
Know I am sorry
You have permanently stolen
A piece of my soul

A Poem by Him

We cannot try, he growled
It is a seemingly hopeless battle
We will never win it
I know you are a good girl —
This is the purest explanation as to why I cannot taint you
I will not taint you
This is a fact
For there is an array of other women to feel
And to touch
And to fuck
I will not try, he declared
There is no need to try
For I know how it will destroy you
And, sweetheart
There's no need to be broken
Because of someone like me

I Still Wait

The train platform
Is broken with cracks and bruises
My foot wanders over one
It is not that I wish for bad luck
I deserve it

My lips feel the saline
They ignore its taste
They instead focus on forming
Coherent and stable sentences
They try and they fail

There is an elderly woman
I wonder how she thinks
I once heard age is a function of wisdom
This is false
It is the child that holds the secrets of the world

When we think of emotions
The spectrum trails from
Happiness to Sadness
I think of the median:
Neutrality has a sour taste

A motorcycle zooms by
It runs over my thoughts
I long for the leather that suffocates
I daydream of this intoxication
With an older man whose hair is too long

I do not know where I am
His hand grasps my thigh
He controls me

I look at him again
I didn't notice his jagged teeth until it was too late

In all, it would be best
To be left alone
I have found this an impossible task
I wait for the train
It never comes

How Do You Feel?

A loaded question
Designed to barely scrape the surface
We never know
What is truly hidden beneath

Do you want the raw and bruised truth?
Do you want the sweatshirt with the cigarette holes?
I hate that we might not say
What you want to hear, my love

I punch my conscience in the face

I fear
I do not know how to please you

I choose to say I feel okay —
Okay encompasses my utter indifference
To all the lilacs and weeds
To all the bluebirds and crows

I ask it back
Your face glistens
I think of a beautiful summer day
I dream of us touching in the ocean

In this fantasy
I plead to the man who enslaves me

I smirk
Not because I am happy
But because I am sick

To this end
There is no point

In trying to break free

I am held captive to your touch
Confined to a world
That is no longer my own

Mommy, Do You Believe Me?

Mommy, I promise
I promise
I met the one

He makes my smile so wide
Mommy
I promise
He makes it all Rainbows and Sunshine
And —
Mommy?
How come you don't believe me?

Mommy
Why does no one believe me?
But he makes me giggle so much
And he tells me I'm the only
Girl
In the world

Mommy
I'm the only one!
I've never been the only one before

Mommy
He also told me
I was so beautiful
And so perfect
Mommy how pretty are those words!
I'm
Perfect

Darling, doesn't he have a wife?

But
Mommy
It doesn't matter
Don't you see
I promise
Don't you see
They're so real
The words are so real

Mommy
Can't you see?
I won't be alone anymore
I'll finally be
Free

Lonely Paradise

Falling
Into
A sea

Of
You

I wish
To be
Elsewhere

freedom

a woman in a warm bath with no bubbles
cereal and milk with satellite TV
fresh orchids in the middle of the night

a child's first word
the difference between a clementine and a tangerine
smoke in the air of a campfire

a teacher's prized possession
sweet manuka honey on the skin
grey roots in the center of a black-haired beauty

a heart devoid of injuries
mushrooms on a margherita pizza
the taste of freedom

A Power Plant

Streaks of copper-coated rust infiltrate the entirety of the Universe, of
the Earth, of the Blood
Seeping into my very own frozen heart

Yes, indeed! It is all mine!
In that way, I suppose I am gifted —
I am gifted in the sense I have ice numbing me into completeness,
numbing me into me

What we cannot forget
Is what will happen when the Brain becomes victim to this
harsh winter

My powerhouse, my sanity
Will transform into that of everyone around me:
The robot, the conformist, the antithesis of who I am

Ah, the gift had been a trap all along
A trap that violated me, that used me, that left me alone

But now, alone comprises of something a bit worse
Perhaps, something much worse, something black or something red
It comprises of thoughtlessness, of emptiness

There is a loss of independence
That comes with the rain

God's Word

She screams my name
Though not with her voice
But with her gaze

I need help, she begs
I need help again

I promise you
I try my best
I promise you
I try to be the teacher, the advisor, the friend

I cannot always be the teacher, the advisor, the friend

It's starting again, she urges
I don't want it to start all over again

I try to explain there is no
It
It is only you
It is you that makes decisions
And it is you that allows the voice
To overshadow your rationale

You're wrong, she declares
I am weaker than it

You are what you think of yourself
And there is no more to it
You say you are weak
I agree
But only because you proclaimed it
As God's word

I need you, she pleads
I need your help again

Okay, I say
There is nothing more I can do
Who am I to battle with God?

Futile Rejection

His words manifest into the branches that bar you down
To coddle the glory of feeling wanted
Only to discover
The glass shattered onto the ground

This is an everlasting roller coaster ride
The one that warns "BEWARE OF ENTRY" on every inch of its
rusting steel
The one that tricks you, making you certain that the stomach-
churning flips are about to end
Only to find you are seconds away from the next one

You did not realize what this ride would turn out to be
There was no contract and no preview to lead the way
It was blind faith that threw you into the car
And buckled your seatbelt tight enough to suffocate any chance of
jumping off

Here we are: right in the middle of the ride
Or maybe the beginning or the end?
It makes no difference
You are glued to a life you no longer dictate, but you still try to
regain control

When will you learn that the conductor is the one in charge?
And that the physicist calculated each loop to be perfectly timed?
And that the engineer manufactured the ride to have no end?
There is a reason you are stuck: as a passenger, know it is best not to
fight change

Afraid I

It's never been this bad before

I sob
Tears of tar
While coddled in your arms

Ever feel nothing and everything
At the same exact time?

The Disease spreads
He's now a physical sensation
That relentlessly abuses me

I try to count sheep
But all I see is
Lonely girl
Lost girl
Empty girl

I still shake
Tapping my feet to distract myself
From the atrocities in my mind
Aha! I can no longer hear you

But I only trick myself
I can never outsmart my Master

I try to think of cream-colored flowers
They instantly turn Black in my dreams

Faux security
I thought I found a
Place of Belonging
Only to discover over and over again

I am not the type of creature that
Belongs

Perhaps all I belong to is
Lucifer
Do I at least look pretty for you?

I am tired
Sleep has officially disowned me
The Moon rocks me in His craters
3:52 a.m.
Haziness has become my new religion

I am afraid

Drowning in Blue

My voice cracks mid-speech
A crackle of fire wraps around my particularly destructive mind
It scorches every soft and dreary thought I could ever think
My vision fails
I see only monsters
They are colored in Blue

I am sitting still
But in front of me my body collapses to the floor
Black birds peck away at my lifeless physique
I am in a distant world
As I watch the brutal attack
A spectator of my very own life

I try to reunite with my body
It instantly rejects my attempts
It has already figured out how to create a mind of its own
One that is no longer Black but Blue

Melancholy swoons at my heart
In love with the Blue like no other man
He gives me butterflies
The kind that rattle you
That force you to hold yourself on the ice-cold concrete
To imitate any sense of warmth you once knew

I fall effortlessly into my own rendition of Blue
His touch is enough to drown me
But I do not struggle
I never try to escape
Blue is my destiny

I will always be true to my Blue

Connections and Breakages

Dark blue surrounds us, suffocates us
My feet are massaged by the sand beneath my toes
Your head rests atop mine
Gifting a gentle kiss into the tangles of my salty hair

What a thing to be giddy as an adult
I want to know you
To understand you
To feel you and your body

Logistically speaking
I will probably be
Disappointed
With what I unravel

But for now, it is nice to dream
To run along a vacant beach
Bury ourselves in the whitest sand
And float into our artificial fantasies

Man-Made Destruction II

He looks straight into my eyes
But it's different
He doesn't see me anymore
He's looking past me
A forgotten older time

All I see is
Hollowness
No person
No soul
Exists there anymore
He has been conquered

He no longer sees me

A weight tugs on my soul
Pulls at any sense of livelihood I once held
As he quickly murders me
So sneaky in his ways
I
For one
Didn't think I could hurt anymore

The darkness erodes me
It's nothing new
Just a familiar plague that
Leeches off my light
A recycled Christmas tree
Whose glory has been
Stripped from its bare core

I know
I know I need nothing from you

I convince myself this is true
I convince myself that light is unnecessary for survival
That when your eyes scream
Nothing
As they dart through mine
I will be okay

I will be okay

(Im)morality: A Beautifully Crafted Mess

Our fingers interlock
A rush of electricity finds its home in my body
Desire sparks through me
I smile
But it's nervous
Unsure

My eyes scan the bar
You should not be here
The thought replays over and over again
It's a broken record that ceases to turn off
Deafening my thoughts
Attempting to drown out my furnace of need

It isn't enough, though
You can see it in my eyes
I am hungry

But me, you see
I am a morally stringent being
The epitome of all that is Good
This is what I pride myself on

Why would someone ever be unfaithful?
Temptation is simply a weak reason
A scapegoat
That only the Absolutely Immoral would use as a viable excuse

Yet here I am
Nausea caressing my soul
My gut
All because of me

I have become victim to my body
My mind a tourist incarcerated in a foreign country
For committing a crime so egregious
That I should never be allowed to return to my Homeland
My body indoctrinated this punishment
Specifically for me

I am only human
I was not put on this Earth to be graced with wings
I do not frolic as an Angel
But graze the ground with destruction in every step

The moral goodness that shone through
My saddest, most lonely demeanor
Has shriveled away
I do not know where it went
All I know is that black and white
Have morphed into gray today

My body will not allow me
To lose the feeling
Of your lingering touch
To lose the intensity
Of your crystal blue eyes

What is it you see?
I have no way of telling
A beautifully crafted mess:
I could not have created it on my own

You

You you you
It is so invasive that my individual self has been
Forced to wither out of existence
At first it was slow, like the start of a delicate snowfall
The comfort of the intricate snowflakes landing effortlessly
onto the tongue

Then the blizzard materialized at full speed
It locked me inside of the cabin, alone
The fuel was exhausted
The milk went sour
The bread rotted with mold

You you you
I am bewildered by the power I so easily submitted to
I forgot to put up the fight
I wish I could go back
Maybe call in sick that day
To avoid the inevitable demise of my humanity
that would soon follow
But wanting and needing are two different species

The mind becomes foreign when you surrender control
With this, I cannot be free

Sunshine at Last

The room is sterile
An overpowering white
With grids lining the floor

The doctor hovers over
My joyless physique
He asks if I am sure I want to continue

I pierce into his eyes
I am much more than sure…
The spiders bite my neck

Sparks and stars and moonlight
There is blue in my sight
I think of blackberries and childhood

He then says a name
So foreign to me
I am puzzled

Well, darling
It seems as if the procedure
Has gone exactly as you would have liked

Procedure? I am distraught
There is a distant familiarity
With the name that slithered out of his raspberry lips

From now on you will only think of
Sunshine
Your hurricane has been erased

All Summer Long

The summer was lovely
Thanks for asking
I finally felt the warmth that comes with the sunlight

Now as autumn approaches
I feel the dread of isolation
And the auburn leaves crunching with every last step

I navigate my beautiful surroundings
And I find that they are just that:
Beautiful

But it is when I acknowledge
The glamour of the purple-orange sunset
That I find myself most vulnerable to the trepidations
of the world

It is this uneasy feeling that leaves me hunched over
with nausea and drenched in sweat
I meditate for all the time in the world
Only to find that peace is lightyears away,
unreachable in my own century

It is upon this realization that I swallow the happiness
I once found
On your Upper East Side rooftop
All summer long

Afraid II

I am afraid
So afraid of living
Afraid of seeing
Afraid of being
Afraid of the ghosts that haunt my every step
Afraid of the monsters tormenting me under my bed
Afraid of the sun
Afraid of the moon
Afraid of the stars that mock me as they sparkle up above

I am afraid
So afraid of me
Afraid of you
Afraid of him
Afraid of the existence that I choose to embody
Afraid of the weakness you have forced upon me
Afraid of the feeling
Afraid of the touch
Afraid of the loneliness that strangles me every night

I am so very afraid

Alabama

To the girl so brutally deflowered,

I am sorry to say
That we have been plagued with a grave obstruction of justice
Human liberty and all its fragility
Is now on the line

Today, my sweet child
Every free woman sheds a tear
We are ANGRY with the reddest of rage
At the latest loss of how it feels to be an individual
with authority of her own

They tell us that sensuality is a sin
The woman no longer controls the body
The man has taken over and marked his territory
Robbing her of her right to decide and her right to be

They proclaim that daddy is in charge in this permanent patriarchy
Now I must appeal to only him?
An extra button runs undone
And it somehow becomes all my fault

My darling, I personally give you my word
That the time has come
Where we refuse to allow the narcissism of man
To win this gruesome battle held on our own turf

COVID-19

Better known as the devil
We are living in a world scarier
Than your five-year-old daughter's nightmares

The bustling concrete jungle that is New York City
Is deafeningly silent
A still frame from an '80s horror film

Six feet apart?
Six feet under!
I see no difference

Not enough masks or ventilators
Not enough lives saved or deaths mourned
Not enough competence in the man we call Mr. President

The mundane routine that consumes us each and every day
makes today
No different from the next
No different from the last

We long for the comfort
That comes with true revolutionary change:
A walk down the block, the shake of a hand, a kiss in the park

We took for granted all of the ways that humans interconnect
The feel of normalcy has almost been forgotten
The lights are too dimmed: we are unable to steer through
this plague of darkness alone

Maybe You Know the Answers

Who do you talk to
When you are
Against
Yourself?

It is questions like this
That make my
Loneliness
More lonely

It was a dark storm
That blew my house
Away

These Thoughts of You

I sit here with nothing new to say
I sit here and suffer from these thoughts of you
I have not crossed your mind in months
Meaning I am alone in this isolation
In this constant wondering

I wish I wasn't so alone anymore

My head throbs with disturbing images
My heart hits my chest so loudly that I know you can hear it

I try to find ways to erase it
To erase you
I try too hard — I inevitably fail
I always do

I sit here with the hopes of someone new
In an attempt to muffle the static
To sedate the pain you've created

Sometimes I think it is only I
Who has ever felt the burden of true destruction
A breakage of everything I thought was fact
You, so effortlessly, released me
Like an innocent child popping a passing bubble
That had no business being in his way

But I'm not the silly little girl I make myself out to be
I know this happens to millions of souls
Maybe billions
And perhaps it is even worse
Or dare I say —
Much worse

This disconnect between
What I think
And
What I know
Leaves me suspended in the air
It takes me by the neck
So that I have no choice but to *feel*

I know no truth
Because there is none
All I know too well
Is this pounding in my head
From these thoughts of you

An Attack on the Mind

At a certain point
There is nothing to do but accept your internal narrative as truth
You take the ringing in your ears
And turn it into a song

Sometimes you can't stand it
You feel oppressed
As if no one else in the whole world is able to understand
The screws and bolts that comprise your inner thoughts

You try to use it as fuel
A medium of getting high off relentless injustices
Then suddenly it hits you
You have been lying to yourself

Sometimes you think that there are ways to relieve
this war that ensues in your mind:
Perhaps tears
Or sex
Or academia

You soon discover you are wrong
Laying in this field of misfortune
You stare at the sun
To gain some perspective on the world you are forced to face

Your brain attempts to hatch its weeds
Paving the path of clarity you have been searching for
But you find yourself stuck in the midst of a brutal attack
And there is no real way out

You want to pray for the peace
Of a woman at ease
But you don't and you won't

Because you can never be just that:
a woman whose thoughts roam free

Love?

At the first glimpse of the setting sun
My body attempts to take a break from its bleakest day
It is only you I think of
Hazel eyes and sculpted arms, both finding their ways
delicately through me

With everything I do
I now think of you
I walk to the Le Pain on 88th and Lexington
And reminisce about all the secrets and nothings
you spilled to me that day

I bask in the sun on the Great Lawn
I tried to look extra pretty for you that day
Made sure my hair was as silky smooth as those commercials
Made sure my golden eyeshadow sparkled
just right in the sunlight

But you are so much more than my kinked hair
and blackened eyelids now
I have fallen almost too deep
And this time I cannot figure out how to get out of the ditch
I am supposed to be the most logical being I know

It is now
When all the logic has been carelessly stripped from me
That I know I am in danger
For I love you and I am scared

I love you but I am scared

My Poetry

My poetry is on the brink of collapse every time I pollute myself
My poetry is a growing cancer invading every cell of my body
My poetry is so beautiful I cannot handle it at times
My poetry is the only thing I can truly hold as my own

My poetry pains me
My poetry convinces me that nothing in the universe matters
My poetry tells me that only the tainted have anything to say
My poetry pushes me into a frenzy of needlessness

My poetry isolates me but
My poetry also holds me
My poetry is the only one who knows me
My poetry takes ownership of the sobs stuck inside
the core of my throat

My poetry is my very own revolution
My poetry takes a stand against all the gunk that dilutes me
My poetry is a war on the injustices that never cease
to permeate my soul and
My poetry, most impressively, tries *so hard* to stay afloat
in my drowning sea

Acknowledgements

We'd like to first thank our beautiful family: David, Nadia, and Gabrielle. Thank you for perpetually pushing us to be our best and most authentic selves. It is because of you that we were able to accomplish our dreams.

We'd like to next thank our close friends who have always encouraged us to keep writing our poetry at every stage of our lives. Thank you for sharing your advice and ideas on our poetry and this book. It is because of you that we felt confident enough in our words to share them with the world.

We'd like to also thank our independent editor, Elena Marinaccio. Thank you for helping shape this work into the best possible version it could be. It is because of you that we were able to produce a work we are infinitely proud of.

This collection includes poems that have spanned the past decade, which was only made possible because of this overwhelmingly positive support. Thank you to everyone who believed in us. To many more years of poetry to come.